Meditation

How To Alleviate Stress And Anxiety And Attain Inner Serenity Through Meditation

(A Simplified Meditation Handbook For Alleviating Stress And Cultivating Inner Serenity)

Marcel Guillemette

TABLE OF CONTENT

An Overview Of Mindfulness And Exploring The Concept Of The Monkey Mind 1

An Insightful Exploration Of Mindfulness Meditation 16

Techniques Of Meditation 23

The Principle Of Equivalence" Or "The Principle Of Uniformity 44

The Importance Of Incorporating 5-Minute Meditation Practices 70

How To Meditate 104

Strategies For Cultivating Love And Happiness In Your Life 134

An Overview Of Mindfulness And Exploring The Concept Of The Monkey Mind

Mindfulness is a fundamental, uncomplicated principle. It entails attaining a state of consciousness focused on the immediate time frame. Furthermore, it can be stated that our intention is to embrace and acknowledge whatever manifests itself when we observe the current state of affairs.

He employs the practice of mentally occupying a park bench and observing the passage of vehicles.

Envision yourself engaging in this activity presently. The radiant sun casting its rays upon you, the sturdy iron bench providing steadfast support, and the gentle caress of grass at your feet. The scorching and gleaming pavement located in close proximity.

Begin to observe the vehicles that are passing. There are a lot. It's rush hour. Large automobiles, small automobiles, trucks, motorcycles, and recreational vehicles. Certain individuals are proceeding with caution, while others are progressing rapidly and causing a commotion. Horns honking, music blaring.

Let's stop and think.

Is there any circumstance in which you would suddenly leave the comfortable bench and begin pursuing every passing vehicle on the highway? I'm asking this sincerely. Could you brainstorm any plausible justification that would render the act of dashing into the stream of vehicles and hurling oneself at arbitrary cars an acceptable course of action?

Of course not. Attempting to affix oneself to every vehicle would be exceedingly imprudent, not to mention perilous.

BUT...that's exactly what we try to do, so very desperately and on a constant basis, with our passing thoughts.

We eagerly propel ourselves onto the hoods of those vehicles of thought and firmly grip onto the rear sections of their substantial counterparts, subsequently being compelled along the thoroughfare as a result of our deliberate decisions and actions.

Thus, when examining this matter from a different angle, it may initially appear implausible, but what practical measures can we undertake to address it?

An option available to us is to leisurely occupy the park bench, observing the rapid movement of automobiles passing by. We have no intention of employing a magical solution wherein the cars vanish instantaneously by the mere snap of our fingers. Many individuals hold the misconception that mindfulness and meditation entail emptying our minds, rendering them like barren roads. Not so. That assertion appears implausible. Our objective does not involve eliminating thoughts; rather, we strive to observe them passively and endeavor to avoid becoming entangled in their grasp.

By engaging in the deliberate process of decelerating and directing our attention towards the immediate present, it consequently becomes unfeasible for us to fixate on past events, fret about the future, or excessively scrutinize every fleeting thought. To what extent do we traverse numerous instances, spans of time, even extended durations, while being immersed in a state of bewilderment, engrossed in restless contemplations and excessively scrutinizing past occurrences? In consideration of how our loved ones, and ourselves by extension, could potentially reap advantages, what are the potential benefits that may result from cultivating a heightened state of tranquility?

Our primary focus should be on cultivating our awareness.

Jon Kabat-Zinn, the individual responsible for establishing the Mindfulness-Based Stress Reduction program at the University of Massachusetts Medical Center, articulates that mindfulness entails directing one's attention intentionally towards the present moment, devoid of any judgement.

This approach to experiencing the present moment may appear deceptively straightforward in its simplicity, yet the true test lies in dealing with the cognitive phenomenon commonly referred to as the monkey mind. According to the teachings of the Buddha, it is conveyed that every individual possesses minds akin to that of monkeys. Our minds are filled with a flurry of restless thoughts and attachments, constantly vying for our attention through their frenzied clamor, bustling energy, and overall disorder. And thus, our time is frequently occupied by addressing such uproar.

Engage in the act of leisurely sitting and partaking in a morning beverage. Such a simple task. However, how frequently do we truly take the time to diligently partake in the act of sitting down and centering our attention solely on the coffee, fully relishing its flavor, basking in its comforting warmth, and feeling profoundly grateful for the opportunity to savor such a precious moment? It is highly likely that the situation unfolds in the following manner:

"**settles into a chair while holding a cup of coffee**

Oh no, the screw on this chair is still not secured properly. I explicitly instructed Dan to rectify that matter the previous week. Similar to the laundry I requested his assistance in folding, which unfortunately remained incomplete.

initially sips / finds that the medium roast possesses a delightful flavor

I sincerely hope that I will not be called upon to deliver a speech at the morning's meeting. Mary Ann is highly critical and consistently wears a smug expression on her face.

another sip

Oh, behold the avian creature perched upon the sill of the window! Its aesthetic allure is truly captivating! The azure hue exhibited by its plumage resembles...

sip

Perhaps I will partake in watching an episode of Golden Girls upon my arrival at home. Alternatively, one could consider seeking out a film selection on the Amazon Prime platform. I wonder whether they have automatically charged my Prime subscription fee in the previous month or if it is due to be deducted this month.

savoring / inhaling deeply / embracing a fleeting moment of mindfulness

takes hold of the iPhone device and reviews notifications on the Facebook application

*

We engage in this activity on a regular basis. It is not surprising that a significant portion of our time is consumed by managing stress, anxiety, and feelings of melancholy. It is evident based on the overwhelming volume of tasks and responsibilities that we undertake. It is frequently excessive in nature. We must acknowledge the stark truth that it is we who indulge in excessive self-service, meticulously selecting what to pile onto our already overflowing banquet platters. We assume responsibility for those decisions; life's occurrences, external circumstances, or individuals around us, whom we might be inclined to hold accountable, are not to be blamed.

It is somewhat unfortunate, I must admit, but the profound truth lies in the fact that the greater our awareness of the cognitive obstacles we impose upon ourselves, the more efficient it will become to subdue the tumultuous nature of our inner thoughts.

The primary objective at hand is not attaining perfection, but rather establishing a consistent practice.

Let's get started.

Benefits Of Meditation

Research on meditation has made consistent progress as the years have gone by. It is not unexpected to discover that a multitude of novel studies centering on the advantages of research are being published on a weekly basis. This body of scholarly inquiry and empirical findings has yielded a valuable advancement in our comprehension of meditation and its myriad rewards.

For numerous centuries, meditation has been purported to yield beneficial effects without empirical substantiation. However, contemporary scientific discoveries now bolster these purported advantages. Meditation provides numerous types of advantages, namely:

a) Physiological benefits
c) Emotional advantages
c) Spiritual benefits

These advantages can be classified as the following specific advantages:

Enhanced cognitive function and emotional well-being.

Meditation is not intended to facilitate the suppression of our problems and concerns; instead, its purpose is to aid us in confronting these obstacles with bravery and applying our utmost endeavor to resolve them. Indeed, in the current era, we find ourselves confronted with hardships directly at our thresholds, subsequently leading to easily amplified levels of stress, fatigue, and despondency, ultimately inducing a sense of surrender. All of these challenges extensively test our capacity to address such matters to the utmost extent. Fortunately, the practice of meditation aids us in confronting these challenges directly. It aids in alleviating anxiety, unfavorable mood, and chronic stress that are prone to affect us. Extensive scientific research has unequivocally demonstrated that under uncertain circumstances or heightened levels of stress, engagement in meditation leads to noticeable enhancements in both cognitive functions such as working memory and emotional states.

It eradicates cognitive disruptions.

Maintaining mental concentration serves as one of the driving factors behind the practice of meditation. Empirical studies have established that individuals with significant meditative experience possess a heightened capacity to effectively manage intrusive thoughts, facilitating the achievement of a state of unwavering concentration. Fortunately, attaining these goals does not require years of disciplined meditation practice. Over the course of several days, individuals begin to perceive enhancements in their cognitive capacity.

The practice of meditation has additionally been discovered to exert a beneficial impact and contribute to the mitigation of psychological disorders. As an illustration, conditions such as attention deficit disorder (ADD), depression, and anxiety are all marked by the presence of intrusive thoughts, leading to impaired focus and concentration. Through the implementation of meditation techniques, individuals can attain a liberated state of mind, reducing the likelihood of experiencing psychological complexities.

The size of the brain expands.
Scientific evidence substantiates the fact that meditation contributes to cerebral

growth. It is possible that you might perceive the present moment as sufficient, given your satisfaction with your mental processes. However, this perception is subject to change in the future. Nevertheless, as one advances in age, the frontal cortex of the mind has a tendency to decrease in thickness. By engaging in the practice of meditation, you will be effectively safeguarding and securing your future during the later stages of life, as it is crucial to acknowledge that aging is an inevitable process that we all experience.

Additionally, scientific studies suggest that failure to engage in mental exercise can result in the deterioration of gray matter in the brain. This deterioration may result in a diminished cognitive capacity. Engaging in regular meditation sessions will effectively mitigate the deterioration of brain tissue. Indeed, meditation promotes the augmentation of brain regions correlated with both working memory and attention. Research findings suggest a significant correlation exists between enhanced cognitive abilities and the regular engagement in meditation.

The immune system experiences enhancement.

Through the practice of meditation, it has been observed that not only does one's mood experience improvement, but there is also fortification of the immune system. As an illustration, empirical evidence indicates that individuals who engaged in meditation alongside receiving a flu shot exhibited a higher production of antibodies within their physiological systems when contrasted with the control group who did not engage in meditation.

Additionally, research has demonstrated that the practice of meditation results in heightened activation of the cerebral regions associated with positive emotions. Remarkably, these advantageous effects have been observed to persist even after a cessation of meditation for a duration of four months.

Assist in resolving symptoms stemming from various ailments

Extensive evidence suggests that the level of stress is a determining factor in the body's capacity to combat diseases. This elucidates the reason behind the amelioration of symptoms when an individual engages in meditation while experiencing illness. As an illustration, symptoms linked to allergies, asthma, cancer, hypertension, and cardiovascular ailments could be mentioned. Scholars have additionally demonstrated that meditation exerts a beneficial influence on a range of health conditions. Additionally, evidence indicates that meditation enhances the efficacy of traditional pharmaceutical treatments. Nonetheless, it is important to note that meditation should not be regarded as a substitute for medical advice from a doctor. Nevertheless, it can serve as a valuable complementary practice when used in conjunction with medical guidance.

Decreases fatigue

Were you aware that meditation serves as a superior catalyst for enhancing both mental and physical well-being compared to the consumption of coffee? If you experience a propensity to fall asleep during daytime hours, even after obtaining the recommended amount of sleep, it may be beneficial to engage in a meditation session. Through the practice of meditation, an individual can attain a state of relaxation while simultaneously enhancing their level of alertness.

An Insightful Exploration Of Mindfulness Meditation

Mindfulness is an inherent characteristic possessed by every individual. It's in our nature. Nevertheless, the prevailing environmental conditions, encompassing both professional and personal spheres, fail to foster such a notion. As an illustration, the skill of managing multiple tasks concurrently is in high demand within professional environments, and even individuals who primarily focus on domestic responsibilities such as stay-at-home moms demonstrate considerable aptitude in this area. There is no inherent issue with engaging in multi-tasking, as previously noted, it is even highly valued. Nonetheless, it does impact your state of mindfulness. Envision a scenario where, during your meal, rather than directing your attention towards savoring the taste, appreciating the aroma, and discerning the texture of the food, you consume it mechanically as your thoughts wander elsewhere, preoccupied with contemplating the forthcoming day, organizing tasks, and attending to various household responsibilities. etc. etc. Therefore, it can be observed that engaging in multiple tasks simultaneously leaves no space for the practice of conscious contemplation. This exemplifies the inadequate cultivation of mindfulness in our environment.

As eloquently stated by a renowned teacher, "Mindfulness embodies an inclusive, warm, accepting, and unbiased cognizance of one's internal and external experiences." It is cultivated through deliberate, non-judgmental, and thorough observation of both our internal states and the external environment. By consciously engaging in the practice of mindfulness, one purposefully directs their focus and attentiveness to the unfolding moments of time. Therefore, you can diminish your reliance on automated routines and immerse yourself fully in the present moment of your existence."

The Benefits

In the preceding publication, 'Mindfulness for Novices,' we thoroughly examined the manifold advantages that mindfulness offers. At this juncture, allow me to succinctly reiterate the myriad advantages that can be derived from adopting this practice.

Numerous studies have provided evidence that Mindfulness is efficacious in the clinical management of stress. It is widely recognized that stress is a precursor to various ailments. In addition to alleviating stress, mindfulness meditation has proven efficacy in managing heightened emotional reactivity, intrusive ruminations, depressive manifestations, persistent physical discomfort, acute periods of fear and distress, as well as various medical and psychological afflictions.

"Presented below is a concise compilation of the advantages that can be obtained through the practice of Mindful Meditation:

Sleep disorders
Suppressed Immune System
Diabetes
Rheumatoid Arthritis
Headaches
Assists in promoting smoking cessation
Increased resilience to change
Improved interpersonal relationships
Reduces irritability, anxiety, and combats depression
Improved decision making capability
Enhanced cognitive abilities, including memory, intellectual capacity, and mental functioning
Increased energy
Improved digestion
Reduced arterial pressure and diminished cardiac activity
Improved pain management
Instances of brief duration and infrequent ailments

Elevated immune system functioning and others

The Significance of Sustained Daily Practice

The cultivation of non-reactivity of the mind, inner calmness, and stability can solely be achieved by means of unwavering commitment and rigorous practice. These developments facilitate and enhance your ability to embrace and confront the distressing and disagreeable facets of life. The development of non-reactivity and stability through formal practice enhances our capacity to embody compassion, as we engage in the serene experience of pure unreactive presence. By cultivating a state of heightened consciousness, one can gradually detach oneself from ingrained patterns of behavior, emotional responses, and thought patterns, thereby fostering a more profound and wholesome connection with oneself, one's experiences, and fellow beings.

As individuals, we often find it effortless to allow our minds to drift. We become absorbed in aimless contemplation of the future or the recent past. However, it appears that we seldom permit our minds to fully concentrate on the present moment. Additionally, due to these cognitive disturbances that lack practicality in relation to our current circumstances, they exacerbate our stress levels by inducing feelings of concern, apprehension, unease, and strain. Occasionally, these thoughts spontaneously arise in our consciousness without significant exertion on our part, demonstrating the susceptibility to stress that exists within us—whether perceived or not!

Hence, it is evident that the regular practice of mindfulness meditation holds significant importance in our lives, serving as an effective method to counteract the detrimental impact of thoughtless musings on our physical and mental well-being. Through consistent and diligent engagement in mindful meditation on a daily basis, the task progressively becomes effortless for us, eventually becoming ingrained within us. In the near future, you will be liberated from the grip of uncontrolled rage, fear, apprehension, unease, and tension. Through consistent engagement in the practice of mindfulness meditation, we can cultivate and foster our capacity to reside fully in the present moment.

Techniques Of Meditation

Meditation can be likened to a transformative voyage, and the various techniques employed serve as the means of transportation. Due to the diverse requirements and preferences of individuals, a vast array of meditation practices have emerged, with certain techniques being more straightforward in their approach. The majority of these techniques were originally imparted by mystics of antiquity, spanning back thousands of years, and have since been transmitted through generations of mentorship. Over the years, certain adaptations have been made in accordance with the specific time, location, and cultural context in which they have been practiced. Other iterations, in their pristine state, remain just as fitting in contemporary times as they did two millennia ago. The compilation of methodologies presented in this chapter should not be viewed as exhaustive.

The objective is to sufficiently describe the concepts and techniques of meditation so that individuals with limited or no prior experience can engage in experimentation and discover the approach that best aligns with their preferences. The selection process has additionally been influenced by the necessity to encompass methods that can be executed autonomously, without the guidance or tutelage of an instructor.

Determining the appropriate methodology can pose a challenge. It is important to bear in mind that techniques serve as a means to an end rather than an end in themselves, as they are aimed at attaining a state that transcends technique. Certain educators and religious factions espouse highly assertive positions regarding their methodologies; however, although it might hold some validity that certain forms of meditation possess broader appeal or prove more efficacious for a larger number of individuals, one must not fall into the trap of believing in the existence of an unquestionable or optimal approach. The optimal approach for you to commence with is the one that you find yourself most inclined towards or that resonates with your innate abilities.

It may be necessary for you to engage in some trial and error in order to ascertain the most effective approach for your circumstances. However, it is likely that certain methodologies can be disregarded as unsuitable for your specific needs even without direct experimentation. Alternative candidates may appear readily apparent. For instance, in the case that you are an individual who prefers constant activity and finds it challenging to remain seated for extended periods of time, you may consider engaging in a meditative practice that incorporates physical movement, such as Sufi dancing, t'ai chi, or hatha yoga. However, it is advisable to acquire these methods under the guidance of a knowledgeable instructor. Scholars are frequently inclined towards the Zen tradition of zazen, wherein one refrains from deliberately limiting their attention to a specific object of focus. If you possess a devout disposition, you may opt for the practice of reciting a divine name as a mantra. Individuals who do not have a specific inclination are advised to consider attempting the practice of observing the breath or engaging in the recitation of the hamsa mantra, an alternative technique that employs the breath. Both of these are organic techniques that are well-suited for the majority of individuals.)

After making an initial selection, proceed to conduct a trial of the chosen method. Occasionally, individuals are able to discern the suitability of a technique following a single session. However, unless one harbors a resolute aversion towards it, it is advised to persist with the selected approach for a duration of one to two weeks. Throughout the period of evaluation, kindly observe and record your thoughts and emotions prior to, during, and subsequent to engaging in meditation exercises. Furthermore, it is suggested that you analyze the overall impact that this practice is exerting on various aspects of your everyday existence. If, at large, you experience an overall improvement in your well-being and consequential enhancement in other aspects of your life subsequent to engaging in meditation, it would be advisable to persevere with this approach. If that is not the case, endeavor to explore alternative techniques until you discover one that brings you satisfaction. After identifying a suitable approach, your progress will accelerate significantly if you persist with it rather than persistently engaging in trial and error.

Breath-awareness techniques

In respiration lies existence, and in certain linguistic systems, such as Sanskrit, the term denoting 'breath' concurrently signifies 'existence' or 'essence'. The respiration patterns of an individual are intrinsically linked to their psychological disposition and overall physiological and cognitive state. For instance, in a state of relaxation, an individual's respiration assumes a smooth, regular pattern characterized by a relatively slow pace. However, in moments of anger or agitation, the breathing becomes audibly turbulent, irregular, and accelerated. During instances of intense focus or when exerting significant physical energy, it is inherent for individuals to naturally retain their breath. The correlation between respiration and mental and physical conditions has been acknowledged in the majority of societies, several of which have deliberately employed breath regulation to evoke certain mental states and enhance wellness.

For instance, within the domain of healthcare, breathing exercises are extensively employed as a component of stress management protocols. In addition, expectant mothers are instructed in specific breathing techniques to facilitate the birthing process. The regulation of respiration holds significant significance within the realm of yoga, to the extent that it has prompted the establishment of an entire yoga discipline known as pranayama. The term pranayama originates from the Sanskrit language, where 'prana' denotes breath, spirit, life force, or vitality. The yogic technique of bhastrika, which involves breath control resembling the movement of bellows, as elaborated in Chapter 3, is advised to be employed as an adjunct for the purpose of enhancing meditation. After engaging in bhastrika, the respiratory pattern will attain a tranquil and subdued state, thus facilitating mental tranquility. The most optimal approach to mastering this exercise is through instruction from a highly skilled and proficient teacher who possesses a thorough understanding of the technique.

The effectiveness of utilizing conscious attention towards one's breath in achieving mental stillness has been acknowledged by numerous schools and traditions that advocate meditation practices. Consequently, several techniques have been developed based on this principle. The primary rationale behind featuring breath-awareness techniques as the initial focus in this chapter stems from their inherent naturalness, general appeal, and proven efficacy. In addition, it should be noted that while these practices may be observed in various ways across different major traditions, the majority of them remain impartial towards religious or philosophical convictions.

The methodologies elucidated in this section confer exclusive emphasis to the respiration as the central point of concentration. However, it should be noted that the practice of breath-awareness can also be employed in conjunction with alternative methods, such as the repetition of mantras.

Specifically, the hamsa mantra, although mentioned towards the conclusion of the section dedicated to mantras, essentially functions as a technique centered around the awareness of one's breath.

Contrary to breath-control exercises, during the practice of meditation, it is imperative to allow the breath to flow naturally, abstaining from any intervention or manipulation of its rhythm. Meditative practices centered on breath-awareness primarily consist of maintaining an attentive state focused on the inhalation and exhalation of breath. Your respiration will naturally transition into a smoother and more regular pattern without any conscious intervention required on your part. One might observe that breath retention occurs spontaneously, or that respiration becomes exceedingly slow and shallow, or that the breathing pattern undergoes modifications during the course of meditation. This phenomenon is completely natural and serves as a positive sign that one's meditation practice is advancing. Nevertheless, if you experience any sense of alarm, it is advisable to cease the activity until you are able to engage in a conversation with a knowledgeable instructor to address the situation at hand.

A guide to practicing meditation through the utilization of breath-focused techniques

Please select any of the following techniques to direct your attention towards the breath. The methodology of quantifying breaths (method 1) can be amalgamated with breath-awareness methodologies that entail focusing one's concentration on a specific anatomical region like the abdominal area or the tip of the nasal passage (methods 2 and 3), or alternatively on points such as the center of the eyebrows, the crown of the head, or the heart.

1. Assume a comfortable, erect posture by sitting either on the floor or on a

chair, alternatively, reclining is also permissible. Please shut your eyes and unwind. While engaging in this meditation exercise, breathe in a natural manner and proceed to count your breaths from one to ten, focusing on either the exhalation or the inhalation. Repeat this process throughout the duration of the meditation.

When thoughts or emotions surface, which they are bound to do, merely permit their presence and subsequent departure, while maintaining your concerted concentration on tallying the breaths. If external noises and distractions are present, it is advisable to disregard them. In the event that your focus becomes distracted and you inadvertently lose track, kindly redirect your attention towards your breath and commence the counting process anew, commencing at the number one.

2. Assume a comfortably erect posture, whether seated on the ground or on a chair, or recline. Please gently close your eyes and cultivate a state of relaxation.

In a relaxed manner, direct your concentration to the perception experienced at the nascent endpoint of your nostrils while the inhalation and exhalation process takes place. Once more, adopt a passive stance towards the thoughts and emotions that traverse your mind. In the event that your focus deviates, delicately redirect it towards the current undertaking.

3. Rather than directing your attention towards the tip of the nostrils, as outlined in method 2, shift your focus towards the rhythmic motion of the abdomen while breathing in and out.

4. Assume a comfortable and erect posture, either on the ground or on a chair, or recline. Please shut your eyes and unwind. Inhale and exhale in a relaxed manner, directing your mindfulness towards the interstices of each breath, the external realm where exhalation concludes, and the internal realm at the core of the body where inhalation culminates. At each of these

junctures, there exists a moment of absolute tranquility.

Maintain a passive demeanor towards mental distractions and in the event that your focus strays, calmly redirect it towards your breath. Through diligent training and repetition, the intervals between each inhalation and exhalation will gradually extend, leading to a state of profound tranquility within the mind.

5. Assume a comfortable, erect posture, either by seating oneself on the floor or on a chair, or reclining. Please shut your eyes and unwind. Inhale and exhale in a relaxed manner, conscientiously attending to the movement of your breath. Endeavor to integrate your consciousness with the breath, attaining a harmonious union and allowing it to guide your every movement. Enter with the intake of breath and depart with the exhalation, pausing briefly within the intervals between breaths.

Maintain a passive stance towards mental distractions and in the event that your focus deviates, calmly redirect it towards the breath.

Multiple alternatives exist to the aforementioned approaches, encompassing techniques like numbering until five rather than ten, directing focused attention solely on the interlude between breaths, among others. One can engage in experimentation to ascertain the most suitable option for oneself. It may be of interest to allocate a portion of your meditation session to the practice of a singular technique, such as the counting of breaths, while dedicating the remaining duration of the session to the practice of an alternative methodology, such as focusing on the breath's flow. Nevertheless, it is advisable, particularly in the initial stages, to determine precisely which technique or techniques you intend to employ prior to commencing the session, and thereafter adhere steadfastly to your predetermined strategy. The act of transitioning from one meditation technique to another is frequently indicative of experiencing a sense of disquietude, rather than suggesting that the efficacy of the current technique being employed is deficient. Subsequently, once you have made a preliminary selection, proceed to execute the methodology for a test period.

Mantra

The recitation of a mantra is perhaps the most widely embraced method of meditation, hence more attention is allocated to this approach compared to others. A mantra is commonly understood as a sacred phonetic composition that individuals engage in through chanting or silent repetition, often employed as a means of contemplation and spiritual reflection. The fundamental essence of a mantra resides in its resonance, while the empirical discipline governing mantras rests upon the capacity of sound to influence individuals and engender varied emotional and cognitive states within them.

Virtually all religious and mystical traditions acknowledge the inherent transformative influence of sound, employing diverse manifestations including hymns, plainsong, chants, and prayers, to elevate and cleanse the spirit, as well as to exalt the divine. The book of St John commences with the following passage: "In the inception, there existed the Word; and this Word, alongside God, was, in fact, divine." A noticeably comparable excerpt can be found in the Vedic scriptures of India, which states: "Prajapati, the supreme Lord of all beings, existed in the initial stages, accompanied by the Word, identified as the transcendent Brahman." It is worth noting that various religious traditions concur on the notion that the genesis of the cosmos was initiated by sound. Contemporary researchers espousing the theory of the big bang - positing that the universe emerged from the detonation of a singular mass of matter -

essentially share an identical perspective.

While the theory of mantra is indeed intriguing, one does not need to resort to either scriptural authority or modern science in order to grasp the immense power of sound. Merely being addressed with derogatory language is sufficient to provoke intense anger and drastically alter your overall disposition. A disconcerting sound resembling the grating of chalk can induce a highly uncomfortable sensation. In light of this fact, it appears prudent to hypothesize that a pristine sound or word is inclined to yield a more advantageous outcome than an ordinary one. Nevertheless, individuals who find this technique of meditation to be efficacious, yet desire to circumvent any connotation of being cult-like or affiliated with religion, often opt to engage in the recitation of a non-significant phrase. There exists a substantial body of empirical evidence suggesting that the repetition of any auditory stimulus engenders a soothing phenomenon, rendering it inherently advantageous. Nevertheless, the extent to which this phenomenon matches the profound impact stimulated by a spiritual mantra remains uncertain.

The science of sound

Sound is, in fact, a manifestation of energy generated by the oscillatory motion of an object or system, and subsequently propagated through wave transmission. Every individual object or system possesses an inherent frequency of vibration, which, in turn, gives rise to a specific wavelength during its vibrational motion. The auditory system of the human body is capable of perceiving waves that fall within a specific range of frequencies. The brain, in turn, analyzes and distinguishes the various frequencies within this range, perceiving them as distinct sounds. Infrasonic frequencies refer to those that are below the threshold of human auditory perception, while frequencies above this threshold are commonly referred to as ultrasonic. While the ear is the primary organ through which sound is perceived, it is important to note that sound waves at all frequencies are in fact received and absorbed by the entirety of the human body. This phenomenon allows for the artistic expression of deaf musicians, who are able to perceive sound through tactile sensations on their skin. The influence of sound on the human body is significant, with certain sounds possessing remarkable therapeutic qualities while others can yield contrasting effects. As a result, several therapists have begun to utilize this phenomenon for therapeutic purposes.

Linked to the phenomenon of sound and vibration is the concept of resonance, wherein a robust vibration can be induced in one system through the vibrations of another system operating at an identical frequency. As an instance, when a tuning fork is struck and a second one with an identical frequency is brought close to it, the second fork will resound by sympathetic resonance, meaning it will emit the same note without being physically struck. In order to prevent the occurrence of detrimental resonance, soldiers choose to refrain from stepping in unison while crossing a bridge. A fundamental comprehension of sound, vibration, and resonance facilitates the comprehension of the theoretical principles underpinning mantra.

The science of mantra

In accordance with the explanations provided in Chapter 2, contemporary physics regards mass as merely a manifestation of energy. Additionally, it posits that the mind and matter are interconnected manifestations of a singular, oscillating energy. The archaic discipline of mantra aligns with this perspective, yet it delves further by examining this energy in relation to sounds, however subtle they may be, varying in their vibrational frequencies. Within the domain of this scientific field, the concept of sound transcends mere manifestations encountered in our routine encounters. Furthermore, it is not a matter of whether it exists; rather, it can be readily observed and encountered across various degrees of intricacy. In accordance with certain cultural customs, such as the practice of yoga, varying sounds are believed to harmonize with distinct energy centers within the human body. These sounds are intricately combined in specific patterns to create what is known as a mantra. It is widely believed that mantras embody the auditory manifestation of the divine entity, with each mantra representing distinct incarnations or facets of the divine. Therefore, the power of meaning is augmented by the power of sound. All of the esteemed traditional mantras possess a purposeful composition, designed to cleanse the physical being and bring about a profound shift in awareness.

The Principle Of Equivalence" Or "The Principle Of Uniformity

The principle of analogy is alternatively referred to as the principle of correspondence due to its portrayal of the interconnection between the individual essence, Atman, and the overarching Universal Spirit, Paramatman. The interrelation exists between the individual realm of mankind and the broader realm of the cosmos.

All the qualities and attributes that exist in God the Father can also be found within each and every one of us. When we engage in the practice of Blessing, we can establish a profound connection with the Divine Energy of the Supreme.

The Principle of Oscillatory Movement

There is naught that remains stationary. All of existence is essentially the manifestation of vibrations that are observed across diverse scales. This straightforward explanation can account for the differentiation between the expressions of physical substance, emotions, thoughts, and various other phenomena. The spectrum of evolution encompasses a continuum of varying frequencies, spanning from the utmost density to the utmost subtlety, ultimately reaching the Divine and Eternal Spirit of the Divine Being. As the level of vibration increases, so too will the corresponding level of manifestation. In reality, material substances consist of energetic particles in constant motion, adhering to a predetermined rhythm. Pythagoras is credited with the revolutionary revelation that movement is an inherent characteristic of all entities and individuals. Objects that may seem still to the naked eye are, in reality, undergoing vibrations at a specific frequency. The cosmological entities observable within the universe owe their existence to the operation of an immortal force of sublime origin. When an object experiences vibration, it can create the illusion of absolute stillness. For example, the rotating spokes of a wheel may give the perception of being a solid, stationary entity. Consequently, it is imperative to bear in mind that external appearances can be deceiving. Alternatively, we should expand our exploration to approach a more accurate understanding and ascertain the inherent nature of an object or entity as either coarse or polished. Through our inquiry, it will be discovered that light, heat, magnetism, and electricity are ultimately discerned as mere manifestations of vibratory phenomena. The aforementioned principle holds valid in the case of an individual's cognitions, emotions, disposition, and volition, whereby all these phenomena encompass oscillating states that can be projected outward and exert an influence, be it significant or insignificant, on the immediate surroundings.

The capacity to interfere at subordinate stages of realization in order to achieve intended alterations is precisely what the law of vibration designates as the capacity to generate.

Through adhering to the prescribed procedures elucidated in the Art of Blessing, we are able to effectively invoke the manifestation of the Supreme Energy within ourselves in conformity with the law of vibration. It is the Divine Energy of utmost supremacy, bestowed upon the world by the Almighty Creator, and imparted to the world by the Supreme Spirit of God. We initiate the initial action towards the attainment of Divine Love by drawing it towards our beings. This energy represents the immediate response bestowed upon every individual by the Divine Creator.

Inquire, and it shall be bestowed upon you. This represents the intrinsic commitment established by the Creator towards the act of creation, an obligation that has consistently been upheld: 'Seek and you shall find.' In immediate and direct adherence to our entreaties, the Almighty graciously imparts unto us the preeminent celestial powers of His Spirit.

The Art of Blessing grants us access to the most invaluable spiritual treasures. The divine energies bestowed by God upon the individual spirit Atman exhibit remarkable frequency of vibration, thereby enabling the manifestation of all phenomena across the entirety of the spiritual realm.

The fundamental doctrine positing that each action yields a corresponding consequence.

Each authentic and enduring cause bears its corresponding effect, while each manifest effect is rooted in a distinct underlying cause that was instrumental in its inception. All events transpire in alignment with the fundamental principles established by a divine entity. The law of necessity is commonly misconstrued and attributed to mere chance or happenstance by those individuals who lack a comprehensive understanding of its fundamental essence. The immutable laws decreed by the Almighty cannot be evaded by any individual.

This particular mindset appears quite commonplace to us, given our inclination to interpret the principle of causality in its most bleak, unfavorable, and ill-fated manifestations. This principle, commonly known as the law of Karma, is often misinterpreted due to our insufficient profundity and mediocrity, thus leading us to confuse superficial manifestations with true essence. Luck and coincidence are concepts that hold no validity. There exists a strong correlation between the occurrences that transpire and the subsequent outcomes. All cognitive processes stem from the realm of the intellect, consequently manifesting into tangible behaviors. Each of these serves as a crucial element within the interconnected web of causality. This enigma is unveiled by delving into the exploration of sacred spiritual principles. Hence, in pursuit of attaining the state of happiness, which serves as a manifestation of spiritual growth, it becomes imperative to undergo the cultivation of the mind. Regrettably, a considerable portion of individuals impose limitations on their own pursuit of happiness, opting instead to fixate on negative mental states. They willingly acquiesce to the preferences of others, exemplified by their engagement with diverse mediums of mass communication. By relinquishing their capacity to exercise independent volition in this manner, individuals expose themselves to the possibility of being easily influenced. A sagacious and enlightened individual possesses the capacity to adeptly employ divine law in an astute fashion, thereby offsetting the statutes devised by humanity. The more advanced entity consistently prevails over the less advanced one. The pervasive emotion of apprehension is a torment that hinders the acquisition of knowledge and impedes the advancement of our species. Consequently, in the event that we encounter uneasiness, it is imperative that we openly acknowledge our mistakes, proceed forward with our lives, and strive to uphold our poise. The errors committed by others are indicative of our own position, while our mistakes do not impact others in any way. When an individual inflicts harm upon us, they contribute to their own karmic trajectory, without exerting any influence on our own circumstances. Consequently, it is advisable not to pursue vengeance; instead, it is imperative to reflect upon the circumstances that led to such behavior being directed towards us. Hence, the principle which dictates "equivalence in retaliation," is no longer relevant.

It is of utmost importance that we regard each of our experiences as a spiritual examination that allows us to recognize our flaws and develop in response to them. If we fail to derive any meaningful lessons from this encounter, we risk lagging behind our peers who possess greater levels of sophistication and advancement. For example, an individual who engages in the act of homicide will be subjected to being slain in their subsequent embodiment. In light of his actions, it is incumbent upon him to prioritize his own well-being. Failure to understand this concept will result in a perpetual cycle of interpersonal violence and victimization. Consequently, it is imperative for us to develop self-awareness, to exhibit integrity and objectivity towards ourselves, to strive for spiritual enlightenment, and to embark on a journey that ultimately culminates in attaining celestial blessings, as we ascend towards a higher plane of existence. Each phenomenon is a product of underlying factors, of which our knowledge is confined; nonetheless, once the enigma is unraveled, the occurrences become entirely foreseeable.

The Principle of Synchronicity and Timing

There exists a solitary deity, which encompasses the entirety of creation in a harmonious convergence. This encompasses all constituents, encompassing individuals such as myself, you, her, numerous living organisms, and various appealing elements, among others. Only a level of awareness that transcends the confines of the intellect could conceivably possess the capacity to apprehend this truth. Attaining such a profound state of genuine harmony is unattainable through exclusive dependence on one's mechanical comprehension. The individual who attains such a state of awareness surpasses the actions of those around them and transcends the concept of karma. Individuals who exhibit selfish behavior serve as illustrations of their misguided understanding of life, given that external manifestations can often diverge significantly from underlying realities. It is imperative to acquire transcendent wisdom in order to behold life in its true essence.

The practice of bestowing blessings upon others allows for the awakening of the Divine Consciousness within us. The individual formulates a system of ethics which thereafter precludes him from causing harm to any other individual or entity. Attaining the Supreme goal through Divine Consciousness ensures an unshakable serenity of mind, impervious to any disruption, offering the most expeditious route to achieving it. In regards to commitment, the affection displayed by an enlightened individual surpasses that of a maternal figure. This phenomenon arises as a result of the mother undergoing a perception of detachment from her offspring, while the love of an enlightened individual remains incessantly connected to the divine.

As it is paramount for us to approach the Supreme Divine Reality, we must diligently engage in the practice of the Art of Blessing. The Almighty is the ineffable Being that surpasses all that is within our perceptual realm.

The acquisition of knowledge possesses the capability to negate the impact of causality, commonly referred to as Karma; therefore, the possession of knowledge assumes utmost significance. In essence, it is our profound lack of understanding that serves as the fundamental catalyst for our recurring rebirths. Alternatively, if we can successfully eliminate all of our desires, we will effectively bring an end to the perpetual cycle of rebirth and cease from further incarnations.

Creation encompasses an inexhaustible range of the fundamental nature of beings, objects, and events; yet, as sentient entities, we possess a hierarchy of relevance above all other constituents within this cosmos. Notwithstanding, the entity responsible for the creation of this defies categorization in any manner. He exceeds our capacity for comprehending through rational means, which is why we categorize Him as transcendental. He manifests His presence through the proficient application of the Art of

Blessing, as well as through any alternative efficacious approach whereby the Self is unveiled in connection to the Supreme Consciousness. Should our aspiration come to fruition, it is envisaged that the awareness of His presence will effectively eradicate every manifestation of human anguish. Each mistake has the potential to be rectified and every injury holds the possibility of being restored by a mere infusion of celestial benevolence. The state of being liberated from all desires grants us ultimate tranquility, complete contentment within ourselves, and internal harmonization. Through the application of the methodology of bestowing blessings, we are endowed with the capacity to attain an understanding of the divine essence as "Sat – Chit – Ananda." This profound art facilitates our communion with the divine and fosters our ability to access the elevated state of eternal existence, heightened awareness, and perpetual serenity. It provides a comprehensive exposition, delineating the precise trajectory and methods to attain the ultimate realization of the Supreme Being. Nevertheless, in order to attain divine grace, exertion of some kind is necessary. He facilitates our access to the Art of Blessing as a direct pathway to connect with Him, yet genuine comprehension of His essence can only be attained through ongoing, personal dedication.

Determine the Efficacy of Your Self-Hypnosis Practice

There are several minor physical indicators one can observe to determine the effectiveness of hypnosis, particularly for those who are new to self-hypnosis.

Place both of your hands in close proximity, firmly clasping them together with the palms facing each other, while maintaining this configuration throughout the duration of your hypnotic state. Envision a scenario where your hands are firmly attached together, as if they have been affixed with a strong adhesive, and continue to assert that it is impossible for your hands to separate. They are stuck together". Now attempt to separate them. If you are unable to do so, then you are exhibiting the appropriate level of hypnosis.

An alternative approach to assessing the efficacy of your self-hypnosis involves focusing on the gradual increase in weight perception in one of your arms over the course of your session. Envision a substantial load being placed upon your limb, thus impeding its elevation. Now, make an attempt to elevate your arm upwards. Should you encounter difficulties in the execution of this task, it can be inferred that you have achieved the optimal state of hypnosis.

What steps to take in case self-hypnosis proves ineffective

Have you ever experienced the frustration of being unable to recall a name that is on the tip of your tongue? As one endeavors to recollect the name, it becomes increasingly arduous to retain it in memory. Subsequently, as you unwind, the appellation naturally resurfaces within your memory.

Common Errors Frequently Committed by Individuals

Acquiring the skill of self-hypnosis does not present a significant challenge; nonetheless, novice individuals may tend to make inadvertent errors. Nevertheless, endeavor to refrain from committing the subsequent novice blunders as you embark on the journey of acquiring self-hypnosis skills, thereby propelling yourself towards a remarkable commencement: "

Having excessive expectations Demanding excessively Setting unrealistic expectations Anticipating an excessive amount

A significant number of individuals hold the belief that self-hypnosis possesses miraculous curative properties, and thus experience a sense of disillusionment if they fail to achieve the desired outcome during their initial endeavor. Do not anticipate attaining your objective through only one or two sessions, particularly if you are a novice. It is imperative to grant it sufficient time to yield desirable results.

Inadequate Attainment of Relaxation

It is imperative that you compose your body and mind in order to sustain a trance-like condition. Engaging in consistent meditation practices will facilitate the acquisition of the necessary level of concentration to effectively employ self-hypnosis techniques.

Lack of receptiveness to the self-hypnosis encounter.

It is necessary to address any psychological barriers one may have towards hypnosis prior to undertaking a hypnotic session.

Insufficient advance preparation

Hypnotherapy requires a significant investment of time and careful preparation in order to effectively utilize it as a therapeutic instrument. It is imperative to note that, akin to any other acquired proficiency, mastery of self-hypnosis necessitates instruction and diligent training to effectively execute and achieve the desired benefits.

Strategies for Actualizing Your Optimum Potential via Self-Hypnosis

Maintain Adequate Hydration

It is recommended to consume water prior to the session to ensure adequate hydration, as being properly hydrated is beneficial for any endeavor involving the clearance of negative energy.

Be Relaxed

Unwinding constitutes a crucial component of self-hypnosis. Through the relaxation of both mind and body, one paves the path for the arrival of substantial, transformative opportunities. In order to optimize the benefits of self-hypnosis for relaxation, it is advisable to complement the process with activities such as receiving a professional massage in the comfort of your own home, indulging in a soothing bath for relaxation, or engaging in physical exercise to alleviate tension and stress.

Prevent Engaging in Emotional Turmoil

As someone who is new to the experience, acquiring a tranquil state of mind can be an exasperating and arduous task. Emptying your mind may incite the emergence of various emotions and lead to a state of instability. Make an effort to disregard these emotions and shift your focus towards attaining serenity within your mind.

The final and indispensable point to be aware of, in order to optimize your hypnotic encounter, is that it is perfectly acceptable if you are unable to attain. The world will not grind to a halt, the rising of the sun will not cease, nor will the heavens descend if you are unable to achieve your objectives. Both success and failure follow a cyclical pattern and constitute inherent aspects of our existence.

Therefore, do not become fixated on objectives; instead, cultivate a fervent dedication to them. One must consistently devote effort towards achieving a goal, instead of expending excessive time and energy on unnecessary fretting. In due course, you will unquestionably emerge as the victor.

Why hypnosis work?

The subject of hypnosis remains to a certain extent inscrutable. Given that the entire construct pertains to the cerebral realm and the inherent potency of cognitive faculties, we have acquired an enhanced comprehension pertaining to its mechanisms and the scientific principles that underlie its functioning. Within this context, we shall explore a selection of theories that can reliably elucidate the functioning principles underlying hypnosis. And why can you place your hopes on it with confidence?

Hypnosis influences both your mental faculties and your physiological state.

As previously mentioned, hypnosis is predominantly a product of the human mind, and there is ample evidence to substantiate this assertion. Dr. David Spiegel has presented evidence indicating that cerebral responses differ when the mind is subjected to hypnosis. The MRI images reveal heightened cerebral blood perfusion and enhanced neural activity within the regions of the brain responsible for regulating bodily functions and consciousness, among other aspects.

Hypnosis induces neuroplasticity

Neuroplasticity posits the ability of the brain to undergo modifications and adaptations. The neural link possesses the ability to restore connections, and as alterations occur within the brain, your perception of reality also undergoes corresponding transformations. Repetition is crucial for harnessing the potential of neuroplasticity. As you continue to solicit the efforts of your brain on a recurring basis, the synaptic connections will grow increasingly fortified. It encompasses thoughts, actions, as well as emotions; the greater the degree of stimuli, the more pronounced the activation and interconnectedness of these neurons become. An everyday illustration of this manifestation of cognitive prowess lies in acquiring novel abilities such as swimming, driving, or mastering a musical instrument, wherein, upon mastery, we can adeptly demonstrate their execution with apparent ease.

Through the application of hypnosis, we foster neuroplasticity by employing suggestive techniques aimed at cultivating a state of tranquility, inner harmony, enhanced self-regulation, and similar attributes. It is possible that achieving this outcome may not be immediate, requiring consistent effort. However, through persistence, you will gradually experience a calmer state and notable improvements as your mind and body establish more frequent and enduring connections.

The phenomena of hypnosis and the placebo effect

The placebo effect arises from the utilization of a substance or object devoid of any therapeutic efficacy with the intention of inducing a mental impression or influence. It centers its emphasis on the correlation between the physical form and the intellect. Illustrative instances of a typical day entail the administration of placebo capsules aimed at inducing a sense of enhanced well-being.

In this context, hypnosis operates on two simultaneous fronts, encompassing both the tangible transformations that occur during the trance-like state, as well as the transformations that arise from the influence of belief and faith.

The convergence of neuroplasticity and the placebo phenomenon yields enhanced outcomes in hypnotic treatment.

The Potential Outcomes of Hypnosis

The majority of your cognitive processes are governed by your subconscious mind. Approximately 95 percent of one's thoughts originate from the unconscious mind as a result of independent generation. This is the reason why we are apprehended engaging in undesired behaviors. They have been firmly ingrained within our cognitive faculties as a result of recurring exposure and consistent reinforcement. Consequently, a considerable portion of our fears, concerns, behaviors, instincts, and uncertainties remain submerged in the depths of our unconscious mind.

During hypnosis, our objective is to reframe and invert these cognitive patterns. Consequently, hypnotherapy confers benefits in the realm of subconsciously fostering habits.

The Absence of Hazards in Hypnosis

Hypnosis is frequently perceived in a negative light, as a practice characterized by deceitful depictions of controlling the mind. Dispelling misconceptions through the use of hypnosis:

Hypnosis does not involve exerting control over the mind.

The utilization of hypnosis does not involve obtaining control over someone.

It does not entail any exercises that will result in additional harm or disorientation.

Hypnosis lacks the ability to coerce individuals into performing acts for which they possess no consent.

The portrayal of hypnosis in a negative manner is not novel. The rationale behind this is the inadequate comprehension of the procedure. This can also be attributed to the apprehension of unfamiliarity, that which escapes our comprehension. We fear!

Within this setting, your cognitive faculties are concentrated, engaged, and effectively regulated. So, what it essentially does is enhance your receptivity and vulnerability to suggestions. This does not imply that you can be easily influenced or that you divulge your true nature.

The potential hazard associated with practitioner recommendations—This is not a risk inherent to the practice itself, but rather a precautionary advisory urging vigilance towards fraudulent practitioners. It is highly advisable and strongly recommended to procure the services of an experienced practitioner for any consultations.

The Importance Of Incorporating 5-Minute Meditation Practices

As previously highlighted in the introduction, chronic stress has emerged as a significant fatality in the occupational setting. Let us delve into the gravity of this silent adversary, with the intent of illuminating the vital role meditation plays as an essential component of a hectic existence.

There are various manners in which stress can manifest in individuals who excessively dedicate themselves to work. Let us examine these manifestations in light of the characteristics they may display:

Emotional

An individual who is experiencing stress may exhibit overt displays of heightened emotions and a deep sense of melancholy while in the workplace. They have a tendency to become progressively dissatisfied with their own performance in work-related matters and display heightened sensitivity and aggression overall. Frequently, they display a tendency towards social withdrawal and demonstrate highly contrasting mood fluctuations which can be considered unsettling. They exhibit a significantly diminished level of motivation and a notable decrease in confidence. The mere fact that they exhibit introverted tendencies is not due to an inherent inclination towards solitude, but rather stems from a persistent underlying issue that manifests in a similar manner.

Mental

In regards to the realm of the mind, individuals burdened by persistent stress tend to exhibit the highest levels of indecisiveness and confusion. Their concentration levels are significantly reduced compared to the average, and their memory function is also noticeably impaired.

Behavioral

In addition, individuals experiencing chronic stress will manifest various alterations in their behavior, including irregular eating patterns and a state of restlessness characterized by nervous movements. They might potentially turn to excessive tobacco consumption or alcohol consumption as a means of managing the heightened levels of stress that they inevitably encounter, and it is highly likely that they would be prone to arriving at the workplace later and departing earlier than their typical schedule, for the most part.

If you happen to experience the majority of the aforementioned symptoms, it is highly likely that you would benefit from employing the 5-minute meditation techniques that will be elaborated upon in subsequent chapters of this book. In addition to these readily apparent indications of excessive stress, there are also physiological ramifications that may present themselves at a later point—a circumstance undoubtedly worth averting. Let us examine them in order to grasp the reasons behind the imperative to avoid the development of chronic stress.

The Long-Term Physiological Impact of Chronic Stress

Impacts on the nervous system. You will come to realize that the cumulative impact of the stress you have been experiencing is significantly more detrimental to your well-being than anticipated. If you fail to effectively manage the chronic stress you are experiencing, you could potentially encounter significant levels of anxiety, thereby exposing yourself to genuine risks. Moreover, anxiety serves as a harbinger to a highly disconcerting state of depression. When one is encumbered with such afflictions, it becomes exceedingly arduous to rise from one's bed and fulfill occupational duties, inevitably negating the diligent efforts exerted towards workplace productivity.

Heart problems. If stress is left unmanaged, it increases the susceptibility to a heightened risk of developing cardiovascular ailments. This can primarily be attributed to the consumption of food that is rich in fat and sodium, which individuals seek as a transient solace, apparently mitigating the adverse impact of stress and pressure. Failure to exercise caution may significantly elevate the likelihood of experiencing a stroke over a prolonged period; an outcome that you likely never deemed possible given the demands of your busy, professional life.

High blood pressure. This condition is commonly referred to as hypertension. Elevated stress levels can lead to a significant spike in blood pressure, posing a grave risk due to heightened vulnerability to conditions such as stroke, heart failure, kidney failure, and heart disease. Elevated blood pressure is a common physiological response to short-term stress. However, when stress persists over an extended duration, it poses a significant concern. Chronic stress has the potential to induce hypertension, necessitating proactive measures to mitigate this risk in the present moment.

Susceptibility to illnesses. Your susceptibility to a wide range of illnesses is due to the fact that your immune system is compromised as a result of the strain on your mental and physical well-being. In addition, stress can impede the recuperation process of any afflictions one may be experiencing.

Altruism

Altruism is characterized as the compelling drive to extend assistance to another individual, ensuring their alleviation of distress, without consideration for one's own self-interest. It is a conscious and voluntary act that stems from the altruistic regard an individual has for the well-being of others.

The assistant does not anticipate gratitude, reimbursement, acknowledgement, or mutual exchange. There have been numerous instances in society's history where tales of selflessness and compassion have surfaced, one of which is the well-known account of the Good Samaritan from the Bible who rendered aid to an injured traveler, facilitating their treatment and accommodation without seeking any form of compensation. This narrative serves as an excellent illustration of altruistic generosity.

As individuals undergo personal development and maturity, they demonstrate a heightened sensitivity towards the subjective encounters of others. Whilst numerous factors contribute to the shift in attitude, empathy is often regarded as the overarching concept that encompasses and elucidates them. Individuals who possess a higher capacity for empathy are more inclined to exhibit altruistic behavior. Altruism also enhances one's social development, consequently augmenting an individual's capacity for empathy. It is imperative that you bear in mind, nonetheless, that the efficacy of aggression and manipulation towards others escalates when there is an enhanced ability to establish a meaningful connection with them.

Empathy enables individuals to perceive the world and circumstances through the lens of another's point of view, thereby eliciting feelings of sympathy. It further emphasizes that individuals may harbor personal apprehensions that will be impacted by the actions of others. This instills a sense of concern within individuals regarding their ethical conduct. The impetus for assistance is driven by ethical considerations, and it frequently exhibits a greater degree of paternalism when contrasted with altruistic actions arising from empathy. Additionally, it implies that the genuine perspectives of the altruistic individuals might not necessarily be aligned with the recipients of their assistance. In addition, purported moral convictions give rise to a greater inclination to prioritize certain individuals while fostering indifference and aggression towards others. This type of mindset is prevalent among individuals involved in acts of terrorism and other forms of extremism.

Proposed Explanations for Altruistic Behavior

Psychologists have developed diverse theoretical frameworks aimed at elucidating the phenomenon of altruism. They include:

Neurological drive

Despite the absence of tangible rewards, acts of altruism elicit activation in the brain's reward centers. Researchers have observed that altruistic behaviors elicit activation of the brain's pleasure centers.

Biological motives

The principle of kin selection posits that individuals are predisposed to providing aid to their blood relatives to ensure the perpetuation of shared genetic material.

Social norms

The altruistic behaviors of individuals are contingent upon societal expectations, norms, and regulations. An illustration of this could be the presence of the reciprocity norm, a societal expectation that encourages individuals to render assistance to others in return for the assistance they receive, thus prompting them towards acts of altruism. For instance, in the event that a friend extended a loan to you in the past, you would experience a sense of obligation to reciprocate when they request the same assistance in return.

Cognitive causes

Assisting others can alleviate personal distress as it reinforces one's self-perception as a compassionate and empathetic individual. Furthermore, it alleviates one from the anguish and unease associated with witnessing the affliction of another individual.

The existence of genuine altruism remains uncertain, as it remains uncertain whether individuals can engage in activities devoid of any concealed personal benefits. Nevertheless, regardless of the underlying motivation, altruism undeniably contributes to the substantial improvement of our global community.

Aggression

Aggression, as per the definition provided by social psychologists, refers to the deliberate behavior of one individual seeking to cause harm to another who is unwilling to be harmed.

As the interpretation of intent is involved, the perception of aggression can vary depending on the viewpoint, and individuals responsible for such behavior might not necessarily recognize it as harmful. Regardless of the circumstances, deliberate harm is deemed more severe than unintended harm, even if the extent of the harm is identical.

Aggression is commonly understood as solely manifesting in physical forms such as pushing or striking, however, it can also be displayed through mental, verbal, or emotional means. Psychological aggression can have a profoundly deleterious impact.

The delineation and characteristics of aggression that we have ascertained ought to prompt you to perceive that the behaviors we have scrutinized as aggressive in certain circumstances may not exhibit the same intrinsic quality. To illustrate, the absence of intent to cause harm exempts individuals such as a rugby player who fractures the hand of another, or a driver involved in an accident with a pedestrian, from being deemed aggressive, despite the significant harm inflicted. A sales representative who persistently contacts you via phone is not displaying pushiness; rather, they are exhibiting assertiveness. A physician has the potential to administer an injection that may cause discomfort, but their intention is to alleviate your symptoms rather than cause harm. This demonstrates that certain deliberate actions may not be deemed as aggressive in nature.

The Frustration-Aggression Hypothesis

Frustration arises when an individual's intended objective is impeded or hindered in its attainment. An exasperating incident will impede his goal-centric conduct, limit his access to opportunities, and jeopardize his self-worth.

A circumstance that incites unease or disconcerts an individual can be deemed vexing; however, what may vex one person may be bearable for another. The aforementioned factors, namely social class, parental upbringing, early childhood experiences, and economic standing, primarily contribute to this outcome.

The potential impact of biological and genetic factors on the emergence of aggression cannot be disregarded. Nevertheless, these remain under the dominion of a male individual, within the confines of his thoughts. An individual who has experienced a cerebral injury may display aggressive responses to stimuli, whereas a non-injured person would not exhibit a corresponding reaction.

The Theory of Instinct

This theory was developed by Sigmund Freud. Freud maintained that human conduct arises from either a direct or indirect manifestation of the life instinct, widely known as 'Eros', which also serves as the driving force behind the perpetuation of life. Based on this context, aggression was regarded purely as a response to curbing libidinal impulses, thereby signifying that it was neither inherent nor unavoidable in the course of existence.

As Freud furthered his exploration and investigation into psychoanalysis, notably in the aftermath of the Second World War, he became aware of the presence of both the life instinct and the death instinct, in contrast to solely acknowledging the life instinct as he had previously done.

Within his scholarly inquiry, Freud embraced the intrinsic manifestation of aggression and put forth an additional fundamental drive dubbed Thanatos. This drive pertains to the formidable impulse of annihilation or demise, through which energy is channeled to induce mortality, ruination, hostility, resentment, and animosity. It commonly endeavors to exhibit hostility through mannerisms, emotions, interactions, and conduct. Therefore, he arrived at the deduction that the manifestation of aggressive conduct within the human species can be attributed to the intricate dynamics and interplay of Eros and Thanatos. A perpetual conflict exists between the two underlying motives.

Per Freud's analysis, the instinctual force known as Thanatos operates without any form of constraint, ultimately leading to one's own demise. It employs alternative mechanisms, such as displacement, to redirect its energy towards external targets, enabling the channeling of aggression towards others rather than inflicting harm and suffering upon oneself. As a consequence, Freud held a sincere conviction that aggression stems from the displacement of self-destructive tendencies away from oneself and towards others.

Attraction and Love

What factor do you believe shaped your choice of companionship, particularly in terms of friendships and romantic relationships? The solution can be expressed concisely as...proximity. There is a higher probability of individuals engaging and cultivating positive sentiments towards those with whom they maintain regular communication. It is probable that your college acquaintance would consist of an individual with whom you have the same academic courses or reside in the same dormitory. It is also probable that you will establish friendships with individuals residing in close proximity rather than others residing at a considerable distance. The close proximity facilitates relationships, as individuals have increased opportunities to deepen their understanding of each other.

One of the rationales behind the significance of proximity lies in its association with familiarity, thereby engendering a greater sense of comfort and attraction in individuals. Individuals who are well acquainted often experience a sense of security due to their familiarity, as they have a reasonable understanding of what to anticipate from these individuals. This phenomenon could also be attributed to the principle of mere exposure, which posits that the increased exposure to specific stimuli leads individuals to perceive said stimuli in a more favorable manner.

The Theory of the Triangular Nature of Love

The triangular theory of love provides a comprehensive framework for elucidating the impact of proximity on the formation of attraction.

Incorporate meditation into every facet of your daily existence.

Should you experience psychological distress, it is likely attributed to harboring emotional sorrow stemming from past events or apprehension regarding upcoming occurrences. Now, it is likely that each one of us harbors unpleasant recollections from the past and occasionally experiences apprehensions regarding potential future outcomes.

If you allocate your mental energy to reflect upon previous events, you are likely to experience feelings of melancholy, as you allow your emotions to be influenced by irreversible situations that have no bearing on the present moment. Engaging in future-oriented thoughts can lead to feelings of anxiety, as it involves allowing your emotions to react to hypothetical situations that have not yet occurred and are void of existence.

Therefore, it is advised to refrain from making contact with the two fires, as doing so will result in burns. The two infernos represent the current state and forthcoming trajectory. Should you choose to make any contact with any individual within that group, it is imperative to exercise caution, as such actions may result in harm befalling your own person.

The majority of our existence is dictated by our subconscious patterns of behavior, as nearly all of our daily actions are a result of habitual tendencies. Indeed, one may utilize habits either in a constructive or detrimental manner. The employment of habits in a detrimental manner can occur firstly through the development of harmful addictions, and secondly through allowing them to govern and dictate one's life. The issue arising from being driven by your habits is the lack of conscious awareness in carrying them out. Consequently, while engaged in a task, your mind inadvertently embarks on a trajectory through past and present, subsequently leading to a state of distress, anxiety, and depression.

Occasionally, when individuals intend to offer guidance, they suggest refraining from dwelling on the past and instead focusing on the future, particularly your aspirations, as that is what will bring you happiness. I hold a different viewpoint on this matter. Contemplating future outcomes will only lead to concerns and stress.

By "being present," I am referring to the act of concentrating solely on the present moment. This entails directing your attention exclusively to this very moment, disregarding the broader scope of this day, this week, and instead focusing solely on the immediate instance in which you are engaging with these words. This practice is referred to as mindfulness, and acquiring this skill is highly beneficial for one's spiritual well-being and mental health.

What is Mindfulness?

Mindfulness constitutes a form of meditation wherein individuals are expected to exhibit heightened awareness and profound attentiveness to their sensations and emotions experienced in the present moment. This form of meditation can be practiced continuously throughout the entire day, encompassing a full 24-hour period. However, it is important to note that adhering to such an intensive practice can pose challenges, particularly for those new to meditation.

It is my belief that individuals who lived in historical periods prior to the advent of technology exhibited a greater level of mindfulness compared to contemporary society, as their attention and concentration were more pronounced. Regrettably, in the present era, advancements in technology, particularly the internet and smartphones, have diminished our capacity for focus. Consequently, the practice of mindfulness has become increasingly challenging for us.

Presently, we are unable to derive pleasure from the simple joys in life, akin to our grandparents who found contentment in activities such as reading or partaking in meals. In contemporary times, we find ourselves incapable of perceiving our actions through our senses, as we are merely propelled by our subconscious patterns. Consequently, we are unable to afford the necessary attention to our actions, as attentiveness holds significant value in the practice of mindfulness.

For me, exhibiting presence and awareness in the current moment is a cultivated aptitude, as well as an ingrained tendency. It requires acquiring a skill and cultivating a habit.

Tips for Mindfulness

It is imperative to diligently observe and remain cognizant of one's surroundings through the utilization of sensory perception. The ambient temperature in your vicinity, olfactory sensations, tactile perceptions, and so forth.

Devote your focus to the minor details" "Give careful consideration to the smaller aspects" "Place emphasis on the finer elements" "Direct your attention towards the nuances" "Be mindful of the subtleties

Suppose you find yourself in a state of ennui, confined within the confines of your bedroom, devoid of any stimulating activities. This occasion presents an opportunity to acquire knowledge and practical techniques for practicing mindfulness. This can be accomplished by directing your attention towards the minutiae present within your room. As an illustrative instance, kindly direct your focus towards the condition of your bed or the embellishments in your surroundings. Consider the origins of all these entities. Take notice of the visual allure of the various hues, and perceive the ambient temperature of the enclosed space. Engage in similar activities, while making a conscious effort to refrain from dwelling on past events or future possibilities.

Additionally, it is possible to engage in this activity while simultaneously preparing a meal in the culinary space. Inhale the aroma of the cuisine, directing your attention towards the vegetable as you carefully peel it. It is imperative that all of your actions be conducted in a contemplative manner.

"Do not indulge in curiosity regarding your future:

While it is commendable to establish goals and foster aspirations, it is detrimental to excessively ruminate on the potential adversities that may transpire within the next five years.

The issue arises when our attention is occasionally diverted from the present moment due to an incessant curiosity about future outcomes. In light of this, I strongly recommend allowing the future to provide the answers. The answer to what will happen lies solely in the hands of the future.

Practicing mindfulness in one's daily pursuits

Endeavor to cultivate a state of mindfulness while engaging in the various activities of your daily routine, as doing so will effectively disrupt the habitual patterns of your automatic behavior. I will now present to you several illustrations of how one may engage in the practice of mindfulness during various everyday activities:

Eating:

Whilst consuming your meal, endeavor to moderate your pace slightly. Enhance your dining experience by directing your attention towards the flavors and aromas of the meal. Make a conscious effort to observe your plate and appreciate the visual appeal and color of the food. Mentally envision the various stages involved in bringing this food to your plate.

Walking:

When embarking upon a journey by foot, endeavor to take purposeful strides with each step. Every step you take envisions imbuing greater vitality to both your physique and your cognition.

It is also possible to engage in mindful walking by directing your attention towards various elements in your surroundings, such as residences, natural landscapes, vehicles, commercial establishments, and so on. And appreciate the visual aesthetics of these surroundings.

Listening:

In the contemporary society in which we reside, it is regrettably evident that one's perspectives and opinions often go unheard and disregarded. There is a lack of attention given to your words. Each individual seeks to express their thoughts and indulges in the desire to share anecdotal tales and showcase their accomplishments. In the majority of instances, we tend to engage in passive listening rather than active listening when someone communicates with us, thus failing to truly comprehend their message. It is important to recognize that there is a significant distinction between hearing the words being spoken and truly absorbing the intended meaning behind them.

The issue arises when individuals engage in conversation with us, and we fail to be fully present, lacking focus and the ability to establish eye contact, among other related factors. And I believe the issue stems from the tendency of our minds to recognize familiarity when engaged in conversation, causing them to revert to autopilot mode. Consequently, this becomes a problematic situation.

Make a conscious effort to disengage from automatic responses and actively engage in the conversation when someone is speaking to you. Additionally, there are various strategies to employ in order to accomplish this.

Please endeavor to engage in eye contact when engaged in conversation, as this gesture fosters directed attention towards the individual speaking and consequently ensures heightened focus on their words. Additionally, prioritize attentive listening and devote critical thought towards comprehending his utterances, endeavoring to interpret and construct mental visualizations based on the content communicated to you. Furthermore, it is imperative that you empathize with him by attempting to adopt his perspective and view the situation through his eyes and listen attentively as he does. Your attentiveness qualifies you as a proficient listener.

Working:

I am unfamiliar with the nature of your occupation, profession, or the current pursuits you are undertaking in your personal or professional life. However, I am aware that the monotonous tasks you perform on a daily basis induce feelings of fatigue and despondency. There exists a methodology to ascertain the solution to this matter.

Endeavor to remain fully engaged and attentive from the precise moment of awakening. Do not expend your energy contemplating the potentially draining nature of today's tasks, or dwelling on the adversity this day may present. Direct your attention solely to the present moment, and I strongly suggest that, in the morning, you engage your thoughts in expressing gratitude for your blessings, utilizing your mental faculties to their utmost potential.

Suppose you are proceeding to engage in your professional duties, it is advisable to abstain from contemplating the events that may unfold during the course of your workday. Avoid ruminating on matters concerning your superiors, colleagues, or any other extraneous factors. Please direct your focus to the present moment. Additionally, it is important to maintain a high level of concentration and exert deliberate effort during your work, refraining from allowing your subconscious mind to wander to thoughts of the past or contemplate future events.

Is Mindfulness Easy?

As previously stated, mindfulness can be regarded as both a skill and a habitual practice. Similar to any skill, it is crucial to engage in consistent and frequent practice. Now, through the practice of mindfulness, you can engage in 'regular consciousness.' Whenever you happen to find yourself engaged in thoughts about the past or future, I encourage you to promptly redirect your focus to the present moment. Do not indulge in overthinking to the extent that your emotions become aligned with your thoughts.

It is imperative to cultivate the practice of mindfulness as a regular and ingrained habit. Failure to be fully present in the current moment may evoke a sense of unease or dissonance within oneself throughout the course of the day. Alternatively, you may opt to establish a reminder as a means of prompting yourself to reorient and immerse in the present moment.

Developing mindfulness may initially prove challenging, yet it is imperative to recognize that the endeavor is invaluable, as proficiency in mindfulness conveys unparalleled benefits for fostering contentment and nurturing sound psychological well-being.

How To Meditate

In the following chapter, you will be instructed on the principles and techniques of meditation. It is essential to bear in mind that repeated engagement in an activity leads to proficiency. The concept of meditation often evokes connotations of individuals dressed in saffron robes, engaging in ancient practices, or alternatively, a gathering of individuals embracing new age philosophies, all assuming an uncomfortable seated position. Nonetheless, meditation is not inherently concerned with matters of faith or even metaphysics. It pertains to existing in the current moment, focusing on one's own being. Indeed, it does provide assistance to certain individuals in nurturing their spiritual and religious beliefs.

Meditation enables individuals to cultivate mental discipline, facilitating heightened conscious awareness of thoughts and emotions. It entails introspectively analyzing one's self-identity and determining their role within the global context. It aids in cultivating a profound sense of gratitude towards the genuine essence of each fleeting moment. It bears resemblance to our execution of bicep curls, employed with the intent of facilitating arm muscle growth. Meditation enhances and fortifies the strength of our cognitive abilities.

Buddhists have long been acquainted with the advantages of engaging in meditation. It holds greater significance in contemporary times, owing to the increasingly dynamic lifestyles practiced across various nationalities worldwide.

There is no specific location requisite for meditation, however, if you possess the leisure and the ability to establish your surroundings, consider implementing the following suggestions.

Prepare for Your Meditation

Please consider your intended objectives with regards to the practice of meditation. Individuals engage in meditation for a multitude of purposes, encompassing the enhancement of their creative abilities or the deepening of their spiritual bond.

Should your objective merely entail dedicating a few minutes each day in a state of mindfulness, solely focusing on your physical being and minimizing concerns about external obligations, then meditation undoubtedly serves as a commendable endeavor. Make an effort to avoid overcomplicating the justifications for your contemplative practices. Fundamentally, meditation entails the act of unwinding and alleviating one's anxieties.

At a fundamental level, minimal resources are required in order to engage in meditation. Simply locate a serene, cozy location where you can peacefully exist. There are no regulations concerning proper sitting or standing postures. Just be comfortable. If you desire to, assume an upright posture. Assume a reclined position if you do not intend to induce sleep. Please assume a standing position if you are at ease with such a posture. Simply locate that destination where you can attain a state of relaxation. In various settings such as the office, a bed, a couch, or a vantage point offering views of either a forest or the city skyline.

Please ensure that you are prepared and at ease. Please dress in any attire of your choice, but kindly ensure that you loosen your belt to allow for unrestricted respiration of your abdominal region.

Distraction Free Space

In the practice of meditation, it is preferable to seek out a serene environment devoid of any disruptive influences. Please ensure that you power off both your cellular device and the television. By closing your windows, you have the ability to mitigate any potential disturbances caused by external noise. You have the option to arrange your space with fragrant candles, incense, or a floral arrangement. Adjust the lighting to a lower intensity or switch them off.

Comfort During Meditation

Please ensure you maximize your comfort. Please take a seat either on the couch or on the bed. Maintaining an upright posture without rigidity proves advantageous to prevent excessive drowsiness. You can assume a comfortable seated position on the floor, using either a supportive pillow or a well-designed meditation cushion. For a favorable illustration of a suitable cushion, please access the following link. One may acquire a specialized cushion or alternatively opt for a couch cushion to fulfill the same purpose. If assuming a seated position on the floor is not feasible, kindly avail yourself of a chair to facilitate your seating. The objective is to achieve a high level of comfort during the practice of meditation.

Wear Comfortable Clothing

It is beneficial to don comfortable attire during the process of meditation. Wearing garments that are excessively snug or ill-fitting may lead to distractions and hinder your ability to concentrate optimally.

With that being noted, do not let your attire hinder your ability to engage in meditation. You have the freedom to attire yourself however you please. If your garments are somewhat snug, we recommend adjusting the belt region to allow for unencumbered respiration and the unrestricted expansion of your abdomen.

The Optimal Time for Engaging in Mindful Contemplation

The concept of an optimal time for meditation does not exist. One can engage in meditation at any given moment and in any given location. While traveling in a vehicle, riding the subway, commuting on a bus, residing within your workplace, or dining out in a restaurant, regardless of the presence or absence of external disturbances, it is imperative that one remains attuned to their internal state, including emotions and thoughts.

For the purpose of engaging in more advanced and profound meditation sessions, it is advisable to partake in the practice during moments of tranquility, when the surroundings are devoid of any noise or disturbance within your domicile. Determine a designated period wherein you can ensure an uninterrupted state for your meditation practice, during which you will be able to attain your optimal level of tranquility.

Scheduling Meditation

Surprisingly, it is possible to engage in a meditation practice as brief as a single minute. Please access the following hyperlink to observe the step-by-step instructions on conducting a brief yet impactful meditation practice.

The significance of time in order to avail oneself to the advantages of meditation is negligible; what holds significance is the frequency of one's practice, regardless of the duration being as time-constrained or as time-extended as one is able to manage.

If you desire to engage in more intricate and protracted meditation sessions, it is advisable to allot specific time slots in your daily routine for such undertakings.

To maintain your focus on meditation without being preoccupied by the passage of time, you may find it advantageous to utilize a readily accessible timer that will gently signal the conclusion of your allotted duration, whether it be as brief as one minute or as extensive as one hour.

Begin Meditating

Commence by taking a seat on your cushion or in your chair. Please ensure that you are seated in a comfortable manner. Maintaining an erect yet relaxed posture is essential as it enhances focus and facilitates respiratory ease. Adjust the positioning of your legs to ensure your comfort. You have the option to either traverse them or elongate them.

In the event of uncertainty regarding the appropriate actions to take with one's hands, it is advisable to adopt a posture that aligns with personal comfort. You can securely cradle them in your lap, by your side, or adopt any posture that provides utmost comfort. Direct your focus towards regulating your breath.

Tilt your chin downwards. Regardless of whether your eyes are open or closed during meditation, it holds no significance. Although many individuals may find it considerably more effortless to eliminate visual disturbances by closing their eyes, maintaining a state of openness can be equally effective provided one has a designated point of concentration.

Please ensure that you set your timer accordingly to facilitate concentration and alleviate concern about the passage of time. It is not advisable to subject yourself to undue pressure regarding the endeavor of meditating for an hour. If you desire to commence with a more feasible approach, it is perfectly acceptable to initiate your practice on a smaller scale. Merely dedicating a few minutes intermittently would suffice, or even the brief one-minute meditation aforementioned.

It is permissible to maintain a closed mouth during meditation for enhanced comfort, though it is not obligatory. Alleviate tension in your jaw muscles as well as your tongue. Remain in a state of tranquility during the process of meditation.

The crucial element for achieving successful meditation lies in directing your attention towards your breathing, as it serves as the fundamental foundation of life.

Rather than fixating on "not thinking," redirect your attention towards the focus of your breath. There exist individuals who prefer to direct their attention towards the process of lung expansion, whereas select others contemplate the airflow passing through their nasal passages. Irrespective of the facet of respiration upon which your focus resides, ensure that your concentration is steadfast.

Engage in mindful observation of the breath without engaging in analytical contemplation thereof. The paramount objective is to exist fully in the present moment, focusing on each breath without the need to verbalize or depict it. Please abstain from concerning oneself with recollecting personal emotions or articulating the encountered sensations in the future; devote full attention to immersing in each breath. After it has elapsed, proceed to encounter your subsequent inhalation. If you find yourself preoccupied by a thought or emotion, there is no need to distress over it. Simply acknowledge and accept its existence, allow it to pass without resistance, and redirect your focus back to your breath.

After acquiring sufficient expertise in meditation, it will become apparent that one's thoughts may occasionally deviate from their intended focus. This is a commonplace occurrence experienced by many individuals, thus there is no justification for self-criticism. Merely acknowledge and redirect your attention towards your breath. It could be expedient for one to prioritize directing attention towards inhalations rather than exhalations. Direct your attention to the area that presents the least difficulty.

Ensure that you do not overly criticize or be excessively harsh towards yourself. Please acknowledge that maintaining focus might pose a challenge when you initially embark on this endeavor. Refrain from depreciating your worth on account of this. It will yield unfavorable consequences. Do not anticipate immediate life-altering effects from your meditation practice. It requires dedication and a significant investment of time. Maintain focus on your ultimate objective.

Anticipated Experiences During the Practice of Meditation

During the practice of meditation, individuals may encounter sensations such as tedium, dissatisfaction, apprehension, unease, discomfort, or even resentment. This is all quite commonplace. It is imperative that you recognize and acknowledge the existence of these emotions, thereafter directing your attention back to your breath.

One may potentially become entangled in the pressures to meet certain expectations and even question the correctness of their meditation practice. The crucial aspect here is to refrain from allowing the weight of self-criticism into your tranquil realm. It is within your role to observe the situation, while refraining from any form of response. Kindly acknowledge and proceed forward.

It might appear overly simplistic, yet such is indeed the case. Embrace the unfolding of events and acknowledge that the emergence of various thoughts and emotions is a natural response. Provided that you redirect your attention to your breathing.

This constitutes a cognitive development program. Your thoughts may stray nearly immediately; however, do not become upset, simply overcome it and proceed forward. These instances present the opportune occasions for enchantment to unfold. Once the designated time has elapsed and your timer has duly notified you, you may proceed to open your eyes and subsequently recommence the activities of the day.

Beyond Your Breathing

As you persist in the cultivation of this technique and acquire the proficiency to achieve deeper states of tranquility through controlled respiration, you will likely find yourself capable of invoking a comparable serenity amidst a highly challenging circumstance. It will assist you in navigating the challenges and obstacles that life presents. However, it requires practice once again. You will perceive a serenity permeating your daily existence, thereby enhancing the overall quality of your life.

What are the benefits of this for me?" or "How does this contribute to my well-being?

When you envision your thoughts as clouds and your mind as a pristine sky, it becomes evident that an excess of thoughts can lead to a perceptible haze in your mental clarity. It may appear as though you are experiencing difficulty in maintaining focus or clarity of thought due to the presence of numerous distractions vying for your attention. Meditation serves as a powerful tool for purging one's mind of extraneous thoughts that hinder focus and clarity, comparable to the efficacy of a substantial gust of wind from a leaf blower dispersing all intrusive mental distractions. What remains is a celestial expanse adorned by a few unobtrusive clouds, ensuring unimpeded clarity and visual acuity.

During the course of your meditation practice, you will also be honing your mindfulness abilities. Meditation is a highly effective method for cultivating mindfulness. As a result, the greater your regularity in engaging in meditation, the more you will cultivate a strong acquaintance with mindfulness.

In the preceding chapter, I expounded upon the notion that self-awareness stands as a fundamental element towards cultivating mindfulness. This is closely associated with meditation, as the practice enables individuals to amplify their awareness of both their physical sensations and the environment they are situated in. This skill will be acquired with proficiency, enabling not only its application in meditative practices but also in the execution of one's routine activities.

We each have allocated tasks that we strongly dislike engaging in, be it the arduous task of washing dishes or the mundane duty of tidying up our beds upon waking. It is evident that the completion of these tasks is necessary, and frequently, we find ourselves harboring feelings of resentment towards the overall undertaking. As an initial step towards cultivating mindfulness, I recommend making the mundane task of performing despised chores the most mindful experience of your day. Rather than mechanically completing tasks, it is imperative to focus on the physical and mental efforts required to accomplish those chores. This approach demonstrates a highly effective method to cultivate mindfulness in situations that would typically prompt distraction.

One of the advantages associated with the practice of meditation is an enhanced ability to sustain focus and attention. Being attentive can be defined as practicing mindfulness. Once the habitual incorporation of mindful meditation is established, individuals will discover an enhanced capacity to attentively concentrate and actively inhabit their daily experiences. Even while engaging in the most trivial activities. According to a research conducted by Katherine McLean at the University of California (Association for Psychological Science, 2010), individuals who engaged in meditation exhibited an enhanced ability to sustain focus and attention on a task for an extended duration, surpassing those without prior meditative experience.

Numerous additional investigations have surfaced, akin to the research conducted by Katherine McLean, exhibiting a progressive enhancement in mental well-being and lifestyle outcomes through sustained meditation practices. The composure and tranquility exhibited by Buddhist Monks can be attributed to a specific cause - their profound engagement in the practice of meditation. The investigation conducted by Professor Zoran Josipovic examined the neural activity of monks during their meditation practice with the aim of discerning distinctive contrasts in brain functioning when compared to individuals who do not engage in meditation. The findings yielded compelling evidence. The aforementioned research indicated that during the process of meditation, the monks demonstrated the ability to simultaneously engage multiple regions of their brains, a phenomenon unattainable without the regular practice of meditation (Danzico, 2011).

The brain consists of two distinct networks that operate independently, namely the external network and the internal network. The external function pertains to the one that we engage with when carrying out activities that require physical effort, such as participating in sports, creating artwork, preparing a meal, or composing an essay. The internal function pertains to the cognitive processes involved in experiencing emotions, such as engaging with a melancholic film, reflecting upon past events, or feeling frustrated towards an individual who unlawfully occupied our parking space. An individual lacking prior meditation experience would typically be limited to accessing these cerebral functions in a sequential manner. Nevertheless, according to the research conducted by Zoran Josipovic, monks demonstrated the ability to concurrently access the internal and external functions of their brains (Danzico, 2011). Pretty cool, eh?

Now, exercise restraint and refrain from prematurely believing that a single session of meditation will instantly transform you into a highly intelligent and capable individual. This film is not titled Lucy. It should be noted that these monks devote the entirety of their lives to the practice of meditation. It is their daily occupation, consistently performed throughout the day. The efficacy of your meditation practice will require a commitment beyond a single ten-minute session to begin yielding noticeable outcomes. It will require a substantial level of commitment and self-control. Meditation should be incorporated into one's daily routine, comparable to the habitual act of brushing one's teeth.

Consistent engagement in meditation can also bring about an augmentation in empathy. It stands to reason that as one attains mindfulness and becomes cognizant of their thoughts and emotions, they naturally exhibit heightened observance towards the conduct and sentiments exhibited by others. As individuals gain a deeper understanding of their own thoughts and the stimuli that elicit them, it is only logical to infer that others too possess similar triggers. As fallible beings, it is understandable that on occasions where one experiences a difficult day and finds oneself easily provoked, others may also be susceptible to similar sentiments.

Sympathy is a valuable attribute in a society where we frequently neglect to establish meaningful connections with fellow individuals amidst the tumultuous nature of our demanding schedules. Observing a destitute person on the street may evoke a heightened sense of compassion as, rather than averting your gaze and proceeding hurriedly, you have chosen to temporarily halt your progress and acknowledge their inherent humanity. You would demonstrate an increased propensity towards philanthropy and assisting others, as your heightened emotional sensitivity would lead to a greater attentiveness towards the needs and well-being of others. This does not imply that you will be indiscriminately giving money to every homeless individual you encounter or making contributions to every charitable organization, thereby disadvantaging yourself in the process. You will not commence the practice of meditation only to subsequently proceed to a nearby church and devote yourself as a servant of God. It simply implies that heightened levels of empathy will amplify your inclination to demonstrate benevolence towards others.

The practice of cultivating benevolence entails a specific form of meditation known as Metta. While practicing mindful meditation, it is crucial to cultivate an attentive state that encompasses the understanding of one's mental and physical state, and the ability to anchor oneself in the present moment. Conversely, metta meditation entails the deliberate act of directing one's thoughts towards benevolence and compassion, both for others as well as for oneself. To adopt a formal stance, one would replicate the seated position typically associated with a mindful meditation practice, engaging in deep breathing and ensuring mental composure. Instead of solely directing attention towards regulating the breath and achieving a state of mental tranquility, metta necessitates the contemplation of others. This involves considering individuals to whom you hold a significant connection or even extending thoughts of goodwill and benevolence to the broader global community. With this intention, a handful of straightforward sentences are to be recited.

May you be safe.

May you be happy.

May you find relief from suffering.

May tranquility grace your thoughts.

And repeat. If desired, an alternative option is to substitute the pronoun 'you' with 'I' when engaging in metta meditation directed towards oneself (Team, 2018). Mentally envision the intended recipient of your practice within the boundaries of your imaginative faculties. Observe that individual in a state of utmost contentment, indulging in laughter, displaying a radiant smile, encircled by elements that evoke an overwhelming sense of joy. The implementation of metta fosters the cultivation of empathy and comprehension towards others, thereby yielding positive outcomes. Desiring the happiness and alleviation of suffering for others is an embodiment of altruism. The practice of Metta meditation enables individuals to cultivate selflessness and incorporate it into their daily lives.

Engaging in the practice of directing your metta meditations towards yourself serves to strengthen feelings of self-care and value. It is imperative to consistently prioritize one's personal well-being and pursue happiness; nonetheless, these ideals often become overlooked amidst the tumultuous nature of our daily existence. In the contemporary era, our preoccupations and obligations have engrossed us so extensively that we have inadvertently neglected our personal aspirations and desires. Our sole desire is to attain happiness, and yet such a fundamental pursuit can be effortlessly cast aside.

According to the availability of your schedule, select a suitable time during the day to incorporate meditation into your routine, and ensure to set a reminder on your mobile device. Strategically place adhesive notes throughout your residence as gentle prompts to engage in mindfulness meditation. The initial few weeks of establishing a routine can prove particularly arduous as the practice of meditation may appear more obligatory rather than a desired pursuit. Commence with a modest five-minute daily practice, gradually progressing to ten minutes as you become proficient in the task.

Please avoid being overly critical of yourself in the event that your nose experiences persistent itchiness throughout the full duration of the 10 minutes, making it difficult to maintain focus. It's bound to happen. In the realm of meditation, a brief duration of ten seconds dedicated to mindfulness can be perceived as a significant progression. The cultivation of mindfulness meditation necessitates dedication and perseverance, yet the profound transformation in one's cognitive and emotional state justifies the endeavor.

Strategies For Cultivating Love And Happiness In Your Life

The initial measure in cultivating love and happiness in one's life is to prioritize self-love, with a supplementary method being the incorporation of daily meditation into one's routine. Engaging in daily contemplation enables one to prioritize oneself, thereby recognizing the value and significance of self-care. By allowing yourself sufficient time to collect your thoughts and regulate your emotions, you cultivate a heightened sense of self-appreciation. And it is at that moment that one will come to the realization that all positive outcomes effortlessly manifest for individuals who prioritize self-love.

By relinquishing negative thoughts, one allows for the flourishing of fresh vitality. Engaging in meditation and contemplation serves as highly effective methods for replenishing one's energy, thereby enhancing cognitive mastery. The way in which you perceive and interpret events ultimately shapes the course of your life. Therefore, if you desire to cultivate love and happiness, it is imperative to commence by nurturing constructive thoughts and beliefs.

Live by purpose

By engaging in consistent meditation practices, one can acquire the knowledge and ability to lead a purpose-driven existence. In the absence of noise, you shall have the opportunity to unveil your genuine life's purpose. Life can become louder than one desires. If one does not exercise caution, it is quite simple to become overwhelmed by the multitude of tasks and activities that consume one's time. Through the practice of meditation, you will ultimately discover the factors that evoke joy and fulfillment within you. Permit yourself to immerse in the present experience, as it is in these instances when you will eventually ascertain your true self.

Uphold honesty

Meditation imparts the virtue of honesty, extending beyond interpersonal interactions to include self-introspection. Take a moment for introspection and reflect upon the falsehoods that have become ingrained in your beliefs. Do you frequently engage in self-deprecating thoughts, questioning your worthiness of receiving love or deserving happiness? When one consistently indulges in negative thoughts, it not only has a detrimental effect on one's sense of self, but also perpetuates a cycle of misery in one's life. By succumbing to falsehoods, one impedes their capacity to attain love and happiness in life. Meditation enables individuals to evaluate their thoughts and discern veracity from falsehood. When one embraces honesty, there is no cause for shame.

Engage in the exploration of novel encounters

An additional noteworthy aspect of meditation is its ability to expand the horizons of the mind, rendering it increasingly receptive to embarking on novel endeavors. As one's cognitive capacities broaden, they gain a heightened perception of their surroundings. Individuals, locations, and encounters that previously held little significance now possess newfound significance. There is nothing that stimulates the intellect quite like occasionally achieving a state of calm and tranquility. Upon each emergence from a state of meditation, your cognitive faculties become more adept at assimilating novel knowledge. This positions you to embrace pivotal transformations that will soon occur in your life.

By abiding by a defined purpose, adhering to the principles of veracity, and actively pursuing novel encounters, one's existence acquires an inherent ability to attract positive circumstances. Love and happiness may be readily attained by cultivating a regular practice of meditation. If one aspires to lead a more purposeful existence, it is advisable to allow one's internal tranquility to assume control. One gains profound insights into oneself and acquires invaluable skills in navigating the external world by allocating moments of solitude to introspect.

The Art of Harmonizing the Elements through Dance

This particular meditation technique is considered foundational due to its focus on harmonizing the five elemental constituents that comprise our natural constitution. Indeed, every aspect within the surrounding milieu comprises these five fundamental elements. Familiarity with these components, coupled with their refinement, enables an individual to transcend to a higher state within the realm of meditation. Enhancing one's intuitive capabilities and cultivating equilibrium in our everyday existence are among the benefits derived from this practice. These five elements are accountable for the creation of this world, as well as the composition of our mental and physical faculties.

The five elements are:
- The Earth Element is perceived through our faculties of hearing, olfaction, gustation, tactility, and vision. The entirety of our muscular and

skeletal structures are composed of the elemental constituent known as earth. This component is accountable for fostering equilibrium within our cognitive and physiological faculties.

• The Water Element is perceptible in its physical state, and can be both tasted and experienced tangibly. It is a fundamental component of our physical structure, as numerous bodily functions hinge upon its presence. These functions include elimination of waste materials and toxins, conveyance of oxygen to cellular structures, and provision of vital nutrients to the cells, among others. Approximately half of our total body mass is composed of water.

• Air Element: Although the Air Element lacks physical substance, it is still perceptible through sensation and sound alone. In the human physiology, oxygen and carbon dioxide are denoted as atmospheric gases. It exhibits fluidity devoid of any tangible structure.

- The Fire Element: In our physical constitution, the Fire Element manifests as the internal warmth and vitality within us. The fire element governs the functionality of our metabolic system, in which all chemical reactions occur. The maintenance of equilibrium in this component is imperative for the proper operation of our gastrointestinal system.
- The Space Element, also known as Akash or Ether, bestows a sense of expansiveness and receptivity to our consciousness, and resides within the hollow cavities of our body such as blood vessels, tubes, and orifices such as the mouth, ears, nose, and intestines. Essentially, it denotes the area in which electrons undergo motion. Space is likewise interconnected with a range of bodily sounds, encompassing our

cardiac rhythm, respiration, gastrointestinal activity, and the like.

Each of the aforementioned components operates in unison with one another. Any form of disparity in one or more elements serves as the underlying cause of our physical ailments, mental strain, or emotional disturbances. Therefore, it is essential to achieve a harmonious equilibrium among them. These components grant us access to "Prana Shakti," signifying the essential life force energy that permeates both our internal beings and the surrounding universe. Each individual element exhibits a correlation with the remaining elements based on their inherent characteristics. Furthermore, the convergence of certain constituents can result in their mutual annihilation, giving rise to catastrophic levels of devastation. As an illustration, the convergence of fire and water possesses the potential to inflict harm upon the human physique. They are unable to achieve a state of mutual cooperation as the presence of surplus internal heat within the body can induce irritation or inflammation, while an excessive amount of water can undermine the efficiency of the digestive system, resulting in poor digestion.

The following meditation technique will aid you in attaining equilibrium among the five elements within the physical form. Meditation can be done at any time, although it is advisable to avoid practicing it immediately after consuming a meal. The optimal time is consistently in the early hours of the morning:

First Step: Establishing a Connection with the Earth Element

1) Please shut your eyes. Please inhale deeply a few times. Inhale through your nasal passages and exhale through your

oral cavity. Exhale any stress, tension, thoughts, and anxieties you perceive to be present within your being. Detoxify your consciousness from superfluous mental clutter and incessant internal dialogue.

2) Direct your attention to your corporeal being, encompassing your flesh, bones, muscles, and overall bodily composition. You have the capacity to perceive and observe all of this. Fostering awareness in this domain entails directing one's attention towards the Earth Element. The composition of our physical form is composed of the fundamental Earth Element.

3) Permit yourself to experience the inherent steadiness of the Earth element residing within your being. Experience the sensation of your roots penetrating deeper into the Earth, firmly establishing a strong foundation within you.

4) As you begin to sense the strengthening of your foundational roots, any challenge or circumstance in life that induces a sense of unsettlement or instability serves as a means of release. You possess the necessary fortitude and resilience to confront any adversities in life with bravery and steadfastness. You embody the resilient nature of a mighty tree, whose roots penetrate deep into the Earth, rendering it unshakable against even the fiercest of winds.

5) Allow yourself to embrace this profound and intense sense of support, residing within it for a brief period and allowing it to permeate every single cell within your being. This represents a novel encounter, and the present moment presents an opportune juncture to indelibly inscribe this impression onto your genetic code.

6) Allow the sensation of safety and security to firmly imbue your genetic makeup at present. May the recently acquired fortitude be duly documented. Allow these emotions to permeate your being, synchronizing harmoniously with your genetic composition, exuding a sense of ease, elegance, solace, and delight.

Second Step: Establishing a Connection with the Aquatic Element

7) Please proceed by taking a deep breath and directing your attention towards the circulation of blood within your body.

8) The human body consists of a minimum of 80% fluids, which symbolize the presence of the Water Element inherent in our physiology. By fostering the conscious acknowledgment of these fluids, you are facilitating the establishment of a connection with the

Water Element and harmonizing its equilibrium.

9) Moreover, as you establish a connection with it, you shall observe the remarkable agility and versatility exhibited by the flowing water. Achieving equilibrium in the Water Element entails enabling oneself to assume the role of an observer, thereby acknowledging and embracing its inherent adaptability. At present, it is opportune to release oneself from entrenched emotions. Please release anything you are currently keeping within your personal realm.

10) Embrace the concept of adaptability and embrace a fluid mindset, akin to the nature of water. Experience the innate adaptability dwelling within your being. This adaptability will assist you in effectively addressing and overseeing your various daily matters and apprehensions.

11) Embrace the present and fully immerse yourself in the experience for a brief period of time.

Third Step: Establishing a Connection with the Element of Fire

12) Now, reiterate the action of inhaling deeply. And by taking a mindful breath, permit your consciousness to become aware of the inner warmth present within your physical being. By directing your attention to the somewhat elevated and lukewarm sensation within your body, you are concurrently establishing a connection with and harmonizing the elemental force of Fire.

13) The presence of the fire element instills vibrant energy and fosters creativity, facilitating a spirited disposition. While actively harmonizing the Fire Element within oneself, individuals may experience a heightened sense of vitality, liveliness, and

enthusiasm, predisposing them to explore innovative solutions to life's challenges.

14) Permit yourself to assimilate this heightened state of energy and vitality into every individual cell of your physical being, and should any trace of dullness or lack of liveliness persist, simply allow it to be replaced by this newfound vigor.

15) Fully engage yourself in the present moment, wherein your creativity is expanding to an elevated realm, accompanied by fervent vitality. Experience the process of transformation across all dimensions of your being.

Fourth Step: Establishing a Connection with the Element of Air

16) At this moment, it is appropriate to redirect your attention towards your breath and intentionally inhale a deep

breath into your lungs. When you direct your attention towards your breath, you establish a connection and harmonize the Air Element within you.

17) This correlation illustrates the seamless, empathetic, and poised manner in which the AIR element traverses throughout your entire body. This element exhibits profound affection and meticulous arrangement as it permeates your whole being.

18) As the element of AIR aligns with your being, you will perceive an intensified experience of profound compassion and love. Additionally, it is presenting multiple simplified approaches to navigate through life's challenges, all while embracing love and compassion.

19) Permit this newfound energy to permeate profound within every individual cell and tissue within your corporeal vessel, and allow its indelible

imprint to manifest within the very foundation of your genetic composition.

Please relish this moment and the revitalized energy that accompanies it.

Step Five: Establishing a connection with the element of SPACE:

21) Please redirect your attention to your breath and inhale deeply once more. Direct your attention to the cognitive realm while inhaling.

22) By directing your attention towards this particular area, you are not only establishing a connection but also harmonizing the element of SPACE within yourself.

23) This consciousness is establishing a connection between you and the expansive realm of Cosmic energies, serving as a stabilizing force in your existence. There exists an ongoing and uninterrupted transmission of

information from your current dimension to the Cosmic dimension.

24) By expanding your receptiveness to this vast energy, you are intensifying your awareness of your profound connection to the present moment. Your consciousness of existing in the current moment is expanding with every inhale and exhale you undertake.

25) Fully engage in this process with your entire being and assume an active role. Allow this energy to permeate deep within every individual cell of your body. Facilitate the transmission of information in this exchange.

26) Embrace and appreciate the profound connection you have with the element of SPACE.

27) Inhale deeply once more and allow this state of equilibrium to permeate all facets of your being. Express appreciation to the cosmos, your

physical form, and every facet of your being for this splendid expedition.

28) Now, instruct yourself to achieve Balance, Integration, and Alignment. Reincorporate your physical presence and reenter the confines of your chamber. Open your eyes slowly.

Following the conclusion of this meditation, it is recommended to quench your thirst by consuming a glass of water in order to re-establish a connection with your external reality.

Engage in this meditation for a duration of seven days prior to progressing to subsequent meditative practices.

Points of Posture

Allow us to proceed with the subsequent three aspects of posture that necessitate your attention in order to sustain the seven key facets of the Buddha's posture.

Postural Focus - Lengthening your Spinal Column

The seated posture serves to establish a firm grounding on the surface. After completing that particular step, it is necessary to direct your attention towards extending your spine. This action will elevate your position and facilitate the retention of your equilibrium throughout the entirety of the meditative session. Based on conventional customs, it is necessary for one's spinal column to maintain a linear alignment akin to that of an arrow.

With that being said, it can be formidable to fully extend the spine and maintain a completely upright posture from the very beginning. To effectively acclimate to the activity, it is advisable to maintain optimal posture by ensuring that your back remains straight. Make an effort to maintain an upright posture and broaden your shoulders, as this assists in supporting your back.

Nevertheless, if assuming an upright posture induces discomfort or elicits any form of physical discomfort, consider adopting a seated position with additional support for your back or even reclining. With the passage of time and consistent practice, your spinal column will experience enhanced elongation, therefore it is imperative that you refrain from being overly critical of yourself in the present moment.

Posture's Third Point: Position Your Hands at Rest

Moving forward, it is imperative that you direct your attention towards your hands. It is advisable to allow them to rest on your lap. Nevertheless, you have the option of retaining them by your side or placing them upon your thighs. It is commonly believed that by placing your hands in a palm-down position on your lap or thighs, it facilitates the uninterrupted circulation of energy throughout your entire body. By maintaining contact between your hands and the ground, you allow the internal energy within you to be transferred downwards, thereby causing disturbance to the harmonious flow of energy within your body. In order to prevent this from occurring, it is advisable to maintain your hands on your lap or in a resting position on your body.

An alternative approach would be to position your right hand atop your left hand, ensuring that your thumbs make gentle contact, and then allowing your hands to rest in your lap at the level corresponding with your navel. This particular pose generates a sufficient amount of energy and warmth within your body, ensuring heightened attentiveness throughout the course of the practice.

Fourth Aspect of Posture: Achieve a Relaxed Shoulder Position

Additionally, it is important to achieve shoulder relaxation by gently retracting them. This contributes to the development of a robust, streamlined posture and facilitates the expansion of your physicality. Moreover, it facilitates the expansion of your heart, facilitating the smooth flow of energy throughout your body.

It is likewise of significance to address the fundamental composition of your hand and its intricate linkage to your cognitive faculties and the entirety of your physique.

The Constituent Architecture of the Human Hand and Mudras.

According to the beliefs upheld by ancient cultures, it is posited that the human body harbors distinct energy points associated with the five fundamental elements in the world, namely air, space, earth, fire, and water, predominantly located within the hands. In addition, the distinct nerves in your fingers establish connections with various regions of your brain. As a result, when you unite your fingers and hands in various hand gestures, commonly referred to as mudras, you effectively manipulate the five elements and specific segments of your brain. This intentional manipulation facilitates the attainment of desired effects.

The thumb represents the concept of space, while the index finger embodies the element of air. The middle finger symbolizes fire, the ring finger serves as a representative of water, and the pinky finger signifies the element of earth.

While one may opt to rest their hands in their lap passively, they may alternatively engage in various mudras to optimize their practice and achieve its utmost advantages. Enclosed below, I present a collection of exemplary mudras for your consideration, which have been found to facilitate the exploration of spirituality, enhance wisdom, foster mindfulness, and promote robust physical well-being.

Gyan Mudra

This particular mudra enhances cognizance, intuition, and conscious awareness by establishing a connection between the constituents of space and air. In order to execute the action, make contact between the tip of your index finger and your thumb while maintaining exceptional rigidity in the rest of your fingers. Engage in this exercise for a duration ranging from 10 to 60 seconds, or potentially extend it beyond should you possess the ability, during the state of meditation.

Buddhi Mudra

This particular mudra facilitates mental clarity and provides valuable insight into one's dreams, aspirations, and objectives. In addition, through regular and diligent practice, one has the opportunity to enhance their verbal prowess, enabling them to articulate their ideas with unwavering assurance while harmonizing the realms of spatial and terrestrial dimensions. In order to engage in this practice, one must bring the pinky finger and thumb into contact with each other, while ensuring the remaining three fingers maintain a straightened position.

Dhyana Mudra

This particular posture integrates all five elements and effectively enhances focus on tasks, alleviates tension in nerves, and facilitates the attainment of inner tranquility. Furthermore, it enhances your overall well-being. To execute this technique, place your right hand atop the left palm, allowing the two thumbs to make gentle contact.

Engage in any of the three poses of your choosing to amplify the efficacy of the exercise. Now, let us proceed to address the remaining three aspects of the posture in the subsequent chapter.

www.ingramcontent.com/pod-product-compliance
Lightning Source LLC
Chambersburg PA
CBHW050235120526
44590CB00016B/2095